GITA IN BRIEF
THE TEACHINGS OF LORD KRISHNA TO ARJUNA
A CONDENSED MATERIAL OF GITA WITH 700 SLOKAS

NATERI RAMANUJ ACHARYULU

BLUEROSE PUBLISHERS
India | U.K.

Copyright © Nateri. Ramanuj Acharyulu 2025

All rights reserved by author. No part of this publication may be reproduced, stored in a retrieval system or transmitted in any form or by any means, electronic, mechanical, photocopying, recording or otherwise, without the prior permission of the author. Although every precaution has been taken to verify the accuracy of the information contained herein, the publisher assumes no responsibility for any errors or omissions. No liability is assumed for damages that may result from the use of information contained within.

Blue Rose Publishers takes no responsibility for any damages, losses, or liabilities that may arise from the use or misuse of the information, products, or services provided in this publication.

For permissions requests or inquiries regarding this publication, please contact:

BLUEROSE PUBLISHERS
www.BlueRoseONE.com
info@bluerosepublishers.com
+91 8882 898 898
+4407342408967

ISBN: 978-93-7139-597-7

Cover design: Shubham Verma
Typesetting: Sagar

First Edition: May 2025

Acknowledgment

I am thankful to the Lord for igniting the desire in me to express my thoughts on everything I have learnt in my spiritual journey. I thank my wife, Krishna Bai of 43 years who has been an integral part of my journey and has been a source of stability when life hit me hard. I couldn't have achieved any of this without the stellar support and unconditional love from my wife for which I am eternally grateful. I am also thankful to my daughter, Pallavi Sastry, my grandson, Kailash Sastry, and my son, Prashant Nateri who assisted me in editing the text with the restructuring of sentences.

I also thank Mr. Haresh Amdekar, who has reviewed the text and assisted me with the correct English spelling of Sanskrit words.

I thank Blue Rose Publishers who have taken the assignment to publish with the cover design.

I express my gratitude to the Lord as I could successfully complete this book "Gita in Brief ".

I dedicate this sacred book to my Parents and Teachers because of who I am.

N.R. Acharyulu

Foreword

Approximately 5,000 years ago, when Arjuna was overcome by the dilemma of participating in the battle of the Kurukshetra against his extended family and people he had grown up alongside, Lord Krishna persuades Arjuna to do his duty (Dharma). Krishna's teachings in this conversation were compiled into the sacred scripture, The Bhagavad Gita.

The Bhagavad Gita is recited by many and has been taught by sages and swamis for hundreds of years.

I have gone through the teachings of the Gita several times, from various publications and different authors, including the Gita yajna performed by various Swamis and have cultivated the habit of writing down the most significant events and teachings from the Gita and compiled them into "Gita in Brief".

I do not claim to have the absolute interpretation of the Gita; this book only serves to be a compilation of my understandings, with the goal of synthesizing key aspects of the Gita.

In essence, The Gita is a science of personality management and a guide to handle all situations in life. Whether with family, with relatives, in society with friends or with employers and employees, the Gita prescribes the blueprint to handle what life delivers to us, while maintaining within us, a Dharmic (righteous) presence.

A person becomes near perfect if they try to follow the core teachings of Lord Krishna. In doing so, they will finally be able to reach The Lord by overcoming the cycle of Birth and Death which is known as Liberation or Moksha.

Every person should introspect and meditate on the idea of self-realization and answer the question of 'Who am I'?

Perhaps too broad of a question but the answer could be attained through solving for ancillary questions: What is my journey and how can I mould it as per teachings? How can I make my life as pure as possible? How and why should I make meditation and prayer a part of daily life?

Gita In Brief - Introduction

The Bhagavad Gita was the answer to the doubts raised by Arjuna during the Kurukshetra War. Of course, such an answer could not reasonably be synthesized so easily for the human mind. As a result, the doubts of Arjuna were relieved through a series of teachings and parables from Lord Krishna.

Arjuna wanted not to fight the war; he was influenced by the emotions he felt of his friends, cousins, and teachers who stood against him. He forgot his role, responsibility, and dharma, despite experiencing the injustice done to Pandavas by Duryodhana and his persons, and despite the mediation done by Lord Krishna to try and prevent such a war from breaking out.

It has come as a scripture written by the sage Sri Veda Vyasa. It talks about the very life to lead and so is called Jeevan Gita.

Mind is the flow of thoughts developed internally (Antah Karana). Time to time by keeping the mind pure, right thoughts sprout and inspire virtuous deeds.

Gita instructs on management of the mind. To address the Gita in the context of the modern age, change management is a topic that is frequently discussed in the corporate world.

Those who are familiar with the backdrop of the Mahabharata War are aware that the Pandavas prince, Arjuna knew that a day would come when a war would be waged against the Kauravas. With this knowledge, he prepared for thirty years, learning new disciplines, and sharpening both the body and the mind. While others merely anguished at the injustice meted out to the Pandavas, Arjuna trained rigorously and acquired divine weapons to prepare for battle against not only Karna, but also his revered Grandsire Bhishma and teacher Drona. He was seemingly well prepared.

However, we do not know when, where, and how this mind is going to trip. Thus, we must contend with two uncertainties, the ever-changing world and the ever-changing mind.

Who could have foreseen that Arjuna, the mighty warrior, acclaimed to be the best, would suffer a severe psychological breakdown? Confronted with Grandsire

Bhishma, Guru Drona, and relatives of the Kauravas forces on the battlefield of Kurukshetra, he started doubting the very purpose of the war. At this crucial moment, for which he had long prepared, he put down his weapons and refused to fight. The Bhagavad Gita was given by Krishna to a grief-stricken, utterly confused Arjuna, unable to think and act righteously.

The teachings of the Divine Song (the Bhagavad Gita) were given to one who was an extremely efficient and successful person but temporarily succumbed to the worst depressive condition. Many people today are in a similar state. Arjuna, before listening to The Gita and after listening to it, presents two contrasting personalities. This clearly establishes how this profound scripture can transform and inspire a person to attain excellence and even exceed it.

It is significant to note that Krishna did not change the outer situation or setting for Arjuna but facilitated a change in the condition of his mind. The Gita is the highest knowledge of self-management. If you can learn to manage your own mind, there is no situation that you cannot face or manage in the external world.

You can manifest the highest glory. You can make the impossible possible. Do you need greater evidence than Arjuna? Observe his predicament before he received the knowledge of the Gita. Analyse how he was transformed from a state of utter helplessness to become the greatest hero of his time. He did not just make history; he made an epic.

The Gita promises that each one of us can make the change. Thereby, we transform not only ourselves but our entire society.

In verse 6:5, the Gita appeals: Lift yourself by yourself, do not look down upon yourself, do not underestimate yourself. It exhorts: Do not remain in your miserable condition. Don't blame the world for it. Do something.

We are so busy blaming everyone. We are so preoccupied with the negative things that we fail to see our positive qualities, our capabilities.

We can make anything happen. We can achieve anything. Acquaint yourself with the teachings of The Gita, imbibe them, live them, and make the impossible possible.

Shri Swami Vivekanand was enlightened with the teachings of The Bhagavad Gita, and he attended the 1893 Parliament of Religions in Chicago. He addressed the audience as Brothers and Sisters instead of Ladies and Gentlemen, a simple act that reinforced the key ideas of Sanatana Dharma: we are all equal in the eyes of the Lord. His oratory skills and the speech he delivered at the Parliament of Religions is widely regarded as the first widespread introduction of the principles of Bharat to the western world.

Swami said out of 8.4 million species of life, only human beings have the capacity to recognise the Lord (Paramatma) and thus are fortunate. Blessed with this capacity, we must recognise that The Gita is of utmost importance for establishing a just and righteous society.

The Gita is not a book on religion but a book on personality development and management of every situation in life.

The Gita has 700 slokas. What is the crux of this Bhagavad Gita? People in this busy age have no time to go through a book with so many pages to understand its essence. To take out the cream is this attempt.

The Bible and Quran were written by the religious heads, while The Gita was told by the Lord himself. Bharat celebrates the Gita Jayanti as a function.

The renowned scientists: Schrödinger, Einstein, Oppenheimer, Heisenberg, and Bohr have all endorsed that The Gita is fundamentally an instructive guide on personality development. Chief Justice Anil R. Dave said if he were empowered, he could have introduced Gita in the school curriculum right from elementary education as a compulsory subject.

To recognise what is true Jnana and is eternal forever. Salvation is spoken by The Gita.

Religion is for a certain group of persons who make their constitution to their benefit, while Dharma (**Justice**) can be followed by all sections of people. Religion is nothing but its opinion or dictum. Religion speaks for its group of people but does not respect or accept other religions.

Regarding the religions of the world, only Hinduism serves to speak of.

Fought in 3000 BC, the great battle known as the Kurukshetra War, was a battle to establish Dharma and eliminate Adharma.

Time waits for no man and yet Arjuna stood with folded hands in Kurukshetra along with Lord Krishna, and Time was witnessing the conversation between them. Today I am not the time, but a witness, said the Time.

Though Krishna was addressing Arjuna, he was talking to me, the Time, because I represent present, past and future. The questions or doubts asked by Arjun are also relevant to the past, present and future.

If I am there, said Time, humans will have to face these questions.

In fact, Arjun was not asking these questions, but I was speaking through him, as every day in every era has its own Kurukshetra. To face the present and future, turn your attention to Kurukshetra and listen to what the lord was saying about matters and issues that have always troubled you.

When Arjuna saw many of his friends and relatives in the opposite army, he became overwhelmed.

Contents

Acknowledgment iii
Foreword iv
Gita In Brief - Introduction vi

Chapter 1
Arjuna Vishada Yoga 1

Chapter 2
Samkhya Yoga 16

Chapter 3
Karma Yoga 34

Chapter 4
Jnana Yoga 46

Chapter 5
Karma Sannyasa Yoga 53

Chapter 6
Dhyana Yoga 57

Chapter 7
Jnana VI jnana Yoga 64

Chapter 8
    Akshara Brahma Yoga 67

Chapter 9
    Raja Vidya Raja Guhya Yoga 70

Chapter 10
    Vibhuti Yoga 72

Chapter 11
    Vishwaroopa Darshana Yoga... 77

Chapter 12
    Bhakti Yoga 83

Chapter 13
    Kshetra Kshetrajna Vibhaga Yoga 85

Chapter 14
    GunaTraya Vibhaga Yoga 89

Chapter 15
    Purushottama Yoga 92

Chapter 16
    Daivaasura Sampad Vibhaga Yoga 97

Chapter 17
    Shraddha Traya Vibhaga Yoga 100

Chapter:18
    Moksha Sannyasa Yoga... 103

Chapter 1
Arjuna Vishada Yoga

In the battlefield before the commencement of war:

Arjuna saw the Teacher who taught the vidya and his relatives Bhishma, Karna, Duryodhana, and Asvathama. He saw his family members Yudhistir, Bheema, Nakul, Sahadev analyse strengths and weaknesses and conclude that the victory or defeat in the war is on his shoulders. He foresaw the consequences of defeat despite possessing the mighty Divine weapon "Pushpatasthra," he was overwhelmed and lost his self-confidence.

Lord Krishna preached him Gita to build self-confidence and the power of mind not only for Arjuna but also for all the generations to come so long as the creation exists. Lord has removed the weeds of suspicion from the mind of Arjuna and prepared the mind, suitable for cultivation to sprout the seeds of Karma Yoga.

Mind is the flow of thoughts developed internally (Antah Karana). From time to time, by keeping the mind pure, right thoughts sprout and inspire virtual deeds.

Once Rukmini, the love of Krishna, asked the flute, the secret for Krishna to hold it always in his hands. The flute replied that its hollowness has made Krishna be with him.

Those who do not allow worldly matters into their minds, by keeping the mind empty reach an equal state of the lord, the Sarvanta Yami.

Arjuna looked at the massive army in front of him. He had to fight them. The size of the army did not cause any concern for him. He knew he could defeat them all. But how can he fight Bhishma, his great uncle, Drona, the teacher who taught him everything he knows Ashwatthama, the friend he grew up with?

Arjuna saw his teacher who taught him everything and all his relatives Bhishma, Karna, Duryodhana and many others. He saw his own family members Yudhishthir, Bheema, Nakul, Sahadev and analysed their strengths and weaknesses and came to the conclusion that the victory or defeat of this depended on him. How can he fight his hundred cousins? Only because they refused to give what belonged to Pandavas? It did not feel right. Arjuna felt weak and sickened at the thought of killing these people. He foresaw the consequences of the war, and it deeply saddened him. He was distraught at the sight of losing all his loved ones and lost his self-confidence. He wanted to put his weapon down and leave the war.

Krishna told Arjuna that this war is not about him. It was between Dharma and Adharma.

It is Arjuna's duty to fight for Dharma and fight against Adharma.

And those teachings are what we have in the form of The Bhagavad Gita.

You might ask, **"Is _Gita_ relevant today? What can Gita teach you today."** The answer is anything and everything. Gita can teach you anything and everything you need to live a better life. And it is still relevant today because of the nature of our lives.

We are constantly at war.

We are fighting innumerable enemies and facing so many challenges.

We are at war against greed, self-centeredness, anger and jealousy.

We are fighting for our happiness, freedom, safety, and future.

We are fighting procrastination, confusion, complacency, etc.

We are fighting our negative thoughts.

We are fighting our ego.

We need to let our past go to move forward. We need to do things against the wishes of our kids for a better future. And we struggle to do these right things. Because we are confused between right and wrong. We are precisely like Arjuna.

We need to do the right thing. But we don't want to because it is hard. That's why <u>Gita</u> is relevant today.

Gita can teach us what is right and wrong. Gita can teach us why we should get rid of 'I' and how to perceive things differently. Gita can teach us how to live, think, handle our emotions, and so much more. Gita can make our lives better. All we need to do is embrace it and impart it in our daily lives.

On the battlefield both sides of the army took their positions.

The Shankha (Conch) was blown from both sides of the army, which was an indication that war was certain to commence.

Krishna asks Arjuna: What are you looking for?

Arjuna said: I am looking at all the father figures, grandsire, sages, brothers, friends and sons.

Krishna asks: Why are you looking? You know them very well.

Arjuna: True! I am not seeing them for the first time.

Krishna: You also know that all these friends and relatives would stand to wage war on this battlefield.

As mentioned in Vedas, Jivatma and Paramatma are two friendly birds sitting on the same tree.
One bird is enjoying the fruits of the tree, another bird is witnessing his friend

Arjuna: Is there no difference between seeing and knowing? Yeh Madhav! Take my chariot to the centre of the two armies. I wish to see both armies.

Krishna: I will take you there, but O' Arjuna, why didn't you do this before the 'Shankha' was blown?

Arjuna: Because war became certain after 'Shankha' was blown. Now there is no doubt about this war happening.

On the other side:

Bhishma: Why is Arjun headed towards us?

Drona: He seems to be in a dilemma but why this dilemma when Krishna is with him?

Bhishma: Now I am in a dilemma. The warrior who defeated us in the Virat War is attacking the army now, which is unfortunately commanded by me. But, has Arjuna forgotten that the war has not yet begun? Bhishma took his bow and arrow in action.

Drona: Krishna has stopped the chariot.

Bhishma: What is this riddle?

Gita says to establish harmony between your mind and brain within. Once they are in synchrony, there will be no struggle in life. When mind and brain are under control and balanced, you can attain calmness and composure.

Those who are hungry for knowledge will have curiosity and will be inquisitive. They will always look for ways to acquire knowledge. Such is their thirst.

Arjuna wanted to see his opponents that were fighting for Duryodhana. He wanted to gauge the strength of the opposition. Duryodhana is an egotistical man with no regard to the consequences of war.

The human body has three powers:

1.Ego 2. Brain 3. Mind

When there is harmony among these three, it will be evident in one's vision, speech, and expression.

Krishna noticed Arjuna's apprehension through his eyes.

Krishna: Arjuna! We are at the centre of the battlefield.

Arjuna was reminiscing. He remembered a certain incident from his past. Bhishma asked Arjuna to embrace him. Arjuna was hesitant as his clothes were soiled from a long journey and he didn't want to spoil Bhishma's clothes. Bhishma replied that he was eager to be soiled with Arjuna's dust and embraced him. It was filled with a lot of affection and respect. There was mutual admiration.

He remembered one more such incident from his childhood with Drona. When Drona asked Arjuna to go and play upon the completion of their daily learning routine, Arjuna stayed back to continue to learn instead of playing. Such was his passion for learning.

Once, when Arjuna was practicing shooting a target, he exhibited a skill which he did not acquire from Drona. Drona was incredibly surprised and impressed. However, Drona decided that Arjuna would not leave him until he gains mastery of that art.

Beware of Attachment and Misplaced Compassion:

Love and compassion are divine qualities, they make our world beautiful. Love is expressed in many ways. We do so many things for the people we love.

Love is the lubricant of all relationships- between a husband and a wife, parents and children, siblings, and friends.

Without love, our world would be a mechanical contraption.

Compassion is expressed by kindness through words and action. The world has so many people who are different in how they look, how they talk, what they eat.

There are so many unfortunate people in this world. There are so many irregularities in life on how people end up where they do. Not everyone gets the same opportunities. Hence the difference between rich and poor, educated, and uneducated. Compassion is a tool that can bridge the gap for the betterment of so many lives.

Forgiveness is also part of compassion. It comes from understanding that, to err is human, but to forgive is a fundamental human need. But it is less pronounced in some and more in others.

Love is immensely powerful. However, love can sometimes blind us, impeding our ability to be righteous.

When a child is ill, the mother cares to make the child better. That is love and much needed. However, sometimes, love can cloud our intelligence. We are unable to see the failings of the people we love. By being blind, we do more harm than good. Sometimes, we need extreme measures to make the people we love be successful.

There is an expression: 'If you give a man a fish, you feed him for a day. If you teach the man to fish, you feed him for a lifetime'.

Also, compassion can be misplaced. It is called 'Karpanya Dosha'. In Gita, it is used to indicate Arjuna's state of mind, as he is conflicted between fighting Bhishma the person he admired and adored all his life, Drona and other relatives he grew up with who are the enemy in the battlefield. He must be reminded that these people were complicit as they decided to fight for Duryodhana who represented 'Adharma'.

Compassion for the poor is a great virtue. However, it is important that the people that are receiving the help understand the value. One cannot respect and appreciate unless they understand the value of help.

So many parents are conflicted between love and discipline. They both can coexist. They are not mutually exclusive. Children are exploring the world and learning the ways of life. That is why they are called children. It is the adults that have this enormous responsibility to coach and shape the kids. As parents we must give the children what they need rather than what they want. When there is abundance of anything, the value ceases to exist. These are the laws of nature.

Arjuna was conflicted as he was reminiscing. He was filled with emotions as this was one of a kind of war where he must fight the people he loves. He started forgetting his role and responsibility towards his family, society, to protect the dharma being a Kshatriya. Above all, he had forgotten his obligation to his close friend Lord Krishna who had been protecting the Pandavas at every stage and was a mediator to stop the war and ensure that Pandavas rightfully get what belonged to them.

On the battlefield:

Krishna: Arjuna, how long will you continue to look at them?

Arjuna: Let me look at them to my heart's content for I do not know who will be left at the end of this war. O' Krishna! Who am I waging this war on?

And whose lives are we sacrificing from both sides?

The man in white clothes who stands on the white chariot has given me nothing but love. I received unconditional love from him. I used to sit in his lap with my soiled clothes. He was impervious to the dirt on my clothes as he loved me so much. He is my grandsire (Pitamaha).

That is sage Drona who gave me knowledge and taught me everything he knew. He taught me more than he instructed his own son, Ashwatthama. He may end up dying in this battle. The very thought makes me shudder. My throat is dry. My hands, which hold the bow, have become numb. My body shivers more than it did on a cold and a windy day. The Gandiva slips from my shoulders. How can I kill the people I honour and respect? I cannot turn this Kurukshetra into my family's cemetery. Why don't you say something to Krishna?

Krishna: I am listening. First finish what you want to say.

Arjuna: What can I say? I would not build my palace on the corpses of my dynasty. I do not want this happiness which stinks of blood. Shall I kill the teachers I honoured? Shall I aim the arrow at those who taught me the art? I do not want victory at this price. Let alone this earthy kingdom, I do not want heaven at this price.

Duryodhana may have committed so many sins by his actions towards the dynasty and the most egregious one towards Draupadi, but he is still the oldest son of Dhritarashtra (my uncle). Should we destroy everything for the price of land?

O' Lord! Even if we lose everything and serve from the sin of ending the dynasty, even if I win the war, what is the victory worth?

Krishna: Why this lifeless dejection in this hour of trial? Despair is neither heaven nor fame, before you call out my name. Tell me when destruction stares you in the face and truth looks to you for protection and victory, how can you display such cowardice? Strong men do not lose themselves in dejection. Do not succumb to your vulnerability at this hour of trial.

O' Destroyer of Enemy! O' Victorious one! These un-Aryan feelings will win neither fame nor heaven. You will even hate yourself.

Arjuna! Get over this weakness, stand up, and fight.

Arjuna: How can I stand up and fight? How can I kill Grandsire? Or sage Drona? How can I kill these accomplished, worthy, and respected people? Shall I defeat those who taught me how to win? It is better to beg than raise hands in attack. At least I will not stain my hands with blood.

Hey Lord! It is better to win or lose this war. Kauravas stands before me like enemies. I know I cannot live without killing them, but it will not be easy to live after killing them. Are they not my brothers? Tell me?

Krishna: Yes, of course.

Arjuna: Is it all that you can say?

Krishna: But that is all you asked. This war is not to establish relationships or identities. Recognise your duty and decide, because only you can take these decisions. I cannot make decisions to save you from this war. This war is yours and so is the result.

In our daily life as well, Lord who is within us all the time, (AHAM BRAHMA SMI) who creates our bodies and minds for us to function and perform any karma. But the Lord is only witnessing every karma we do. He is not involved in the actual execution of karma. Similarly, the Lord is inspiring Arjuna, reminding his role and responsibility. Lord Krishna has taken the avatar to establish Dharma. He wants Arjuna to fight the war to make justice win over injustice.

Arjuna: I am unable to perceive and act with clarity. So become the guide of my soul. I know I stand between truth and lies but cannot decide on which side truth stands. Guide me, Krishna! Save me from despair. I cannot fight in such a state. O' Krishna! Should I fight or not?

Krishna is smiling at Arjuna.

Chapter 2

Samkhya Yoga

Chapter 2,
Verse 11- Yoga of Knowledge:

O' Arjuna! Those who die cannot be brought back to life. The wise do not grieve for those who live or die. They grieve neither for death nor birth. You talk like a wise man, but your words lack wisdom. Before you grieve, find out if they are worthy of your grief.

Arjuna: Are Bhishma Pitamaha and sage Drona not worthy of being grieved?

Krishna: Would I deny it if they were? Remember one simple truth. It is the soul, which is of essence, not the body. Death is not its end because it is eternal. Its journey is endless. Death is a momentary respite.

The cycle of life is such: A child is born, grows up passing various stages and becomes an old Man / Woman and enters the final stage. Death is inevitable. No one can escape it. This is the journey of the body.

The soul goes beyond that. It moves from one body to another. The journey that ends with death is that of the body.

**Chapter 2,
verse 20 – Death and soul:**

The soul's journey is eternal, the body is left behind, and the soul moves on assuming a new body just like we discard old clothes for new.

The bigger hurdle that a seeker face is that of 'Me and Mine'. It means my fixed notions, preferences, priorities, likes and dislikes, craving, infatuations, sense of security and desire. We label things as positive - negative, good - bad, like and dislike. Unless we are willing to see reality as it is, we will not be able to progress in our spiritual journey, for this alone will guarantee harmonious relationships with the rest of the world.

Each of us have been brought into this world with a specific role to fulfil. For that role, we have been given the sense of Individuality. The problem is not with the sense of Individuality, the problem arises when we begin to think that this sense of Individuality is all there. There is another, bigger Self. Now, I am guided by whatever my senses bring from outside, colour by my perceptions and I feel that 'I am talking', or 'thinking'. Behind this 'I' there is another Self, in the absence of which, this 'I' does not exist.

For instance, we breathe in air, the heart pumps blood, and the food we eat is digested by the process of digestion. If we observe closely, we see that these things are not done by 'me'. Slowly we realise that if the lifeforce is not there, then 'me' ceases to exist.

We can point out life force; it is expressed in these forms. It makes my eyes see and ears hear. Life is an expression of Atman though seemingly two, they are one. The scriptures say 'Jivana Sarva Bhautesh' -I am the life-force in all creations.

The real self is activating, expressing, and motivating the individual self.

For instance, when we are working for someone, we carry out the instructions of our superior. That individual assumes absolute authority, but the fact is that it acts because of the self in us. Self is also called God.

Whatever is happening is happening according to God's will; it is for our good. Spirituality does not mean only positive things. The creation and destruction are concomitant. There are so many things (good and bad) that are happening in the world. God will guide us with what must be done. We should do our part and leave the rest to him.

In the Mahabharata, Shakuni was an antagonist, but, if he was not there, then we would not have Bhagavad Gita.

In the Ramayana, if Manthara was not there, then, Rama would have ascended the throne, and there would have been a different course of events.

The so-called labelled negative elements are kindled and brought out and made to fulfil their roles for something positive that is to come later. It does not mean we do not act on it, rather face whatever comes in the manner of inner prompting and fulfil our karma.

To know that the real Self is behind every other activity of the individual self and creation, a three-fold path is prescribed of Nama, Seva, and Dhyana.

Nama, chanting his name; Seva dedicating everything to the higher power, from morning to evening, whatever I have, I try to remember 'it belongs to him'.

Whenever I fail or forget, Nama reminds me of him. Dhyana helps me in realising 'me to we' at the outer level and 'me to him' at the inner level.

Everything is a gift of self. When I do everything with this bhava intention - it will be done with love.

Chapter 2,
Verse 22 and 23 – Transcendental Truth:

Hey Parth! Why grieve when the soul cannot be destroyed? Why grieve for the destruction of the body? The body is not eternal, it is to be discarded. It is the soul which is eternal.

Arjuna: Will those before us be there after the war?

Krishna: What is being is not being. There never was a time when all of us did not exist. Nor a time when all of us will not exist. Why do you feel that life is not complete? We were, we are, and we will be. As for happiness and sorrow, like seasons, they come and go. Those who are impervious to happiness and sorrow are 'Sthitha Pragya' and are worthy of salvation.

Chapter 2,
Verse 14_ Nature of challenge:

Krishna: O Bharat! Be free from the doubts of killing and being killed. Only those who are born can die. The soul is beyond time. The body is born not the soul. If the soul is not born, how can it die? The soul exists. That is all. It is eternal and does not go through the cycle of birth and death. It is indestructible.

So do not worry about killing and being killed. Only the body dies and even after its death the soul does not die.

Weapons cannot kill it. Fire cannot burn it. Water cannot dissolve it or wind cannot blow it.

**Chapter 2,
Verse 23, "Transcendental Truth"**

Why do you worry now?

Arjuna: O' Krishna! Do I call a soul, Grandsire? Is my affection merely for the soul? Is the white clad elderly man merely a soul and not a body? Is the sage who taught me archery merely a soul? I do not deny that souls are holy and indestructible, but I am talking about the body. Am I not related to these bodies? Souls are not but surely people are.

Krishna! Of course. People are born but extend this argument of yours.

Those who are born will certainly die, why grieve for something that is preordained? Those who are born will surely die but death is not the end for them. This is the ultimate truth, and no one can avoid it. Not I, Not You. Nobody.

Bhishma has the boon of wilful death but still death is inevitable. In this cycle of death and birth, where is the place of grieving? The people around you existed even before this birth in another life, but you do not know who they were. They will exist after this birth, and you will not know. Their existence for you is confined to this birth. Beyond that, it is unknown. Before this birth they did not exist for you. After this birth they will not exist for you. So, Arjuna! Why grieve for a life whose death cannot be changed by you?

Atheists and Theists

In the present world, two kinds of people, atheists, and theists, argue on the nonexistence and existence of God, respectively.

Here let us understand that 'Tattva' means 'That'. Whoever caused the creation pervades everywhere in this universe and in all beings?

A person is made of five elements with its subtle form known as 'Antah Karana Chatustayam' that are Mind, Intelligence, Chit, Ego, and Internal senses.

Jnana senses, Tanmatra (smell, taste, sight, hearing, touch) and five elements (space, air, water, fire, earth) Antah Karana Chatustayam. They are all inert.

Jeeva and the Lord co- exist as friends in the body. Jeeva knows the world on account of 'Triguna' but is unable to recognise the Lord, due to the lack of clarity and purity of Anthakarana (Mano Buddhi, Chitta, Ahamkara).

The practice of training makes them calm and pure. The "NIRVISHYA" state is called purification. Or 'Antah Shuddhi', a basic requirement.

If one is successful in remaining in a meditative state, NIRGUNA- NIRAKARA- then one is sure to recognise by a feel of Tattvam.

If one is aligned with that Infinite consciousness (IC) present in every being or in every object, which is not seen but is felt, it is like energy neither created nor destroyed.

This energy is changing from one form to another. Potential energy converted into Kinetic energy, which is then converted into Mechanical energy which is then turned into Electrical energy that is transmitted through cables to factories and residences for utilisation.

Power is generated (from a Hydro station) from a reservoir where Potential energy is in the water stored, allowed to flow through a tunnel and pressure shaft, which means the Kinetic energy, a mass is in motion. When directed on the turbine wheel, the wheel is rotated, which means it is Mechanical energy, the rotor with windings coupled to the turbine when rotates in a stator (having coils to generate magnetic field), Mechanical energy is converted into Electrical energy that is ready for commercial and residential consumption.

The energy that is changing forms and transmitted is not seen but its effect is seen when it is used in a machine or a household appliance that gives the result for which it is made. The energy used in the operation of the appliance is invisible.

As long as the Infinite Consciousness remains in the body, the energy derived from the food consumed, distributed to the billions of cells in the body and organs for them to function. The body ceases to exist without the brain and the mind.

The moment Infinite Consciousness leaves the body, all the organs will come to a grinding halt. With no growth, the body starts decomposing.

The Infinite Consciousness or soul is the cause of this body's mechanism to work for all actions, internal and external. It remains as a witness to all actions and in three states: Conscious, Unconscious and Subconscious. This knowledge is known as self-realisation.

The person who says 'I' identifies with the body is different from this Self 'I'.

The body dies but the soul (the real self) continues to live. It has neither birth nor death.

There are those who deny the existence of a soul. I challenge them by saying, so many forms of energy in this world can be felt but cannot be seen. For instance, the electric current or the heat of the fire and the fragrance of the flower can only be felt and smelt but cannot be seen. Why can't we apply the same theory to the existence of a soul?

Chapter 2,
Verse 28 and 31: Advice and face the challenge:

Why are you so surprised? There are so many things that are preordained, and the outcome cannot be changed. The death of the body is the ultimate Truth. Why do you want to change the ultimate truth and grieve the loss of something that is inevitable? A human being is a mixture of body and soul. The body is the vehicle for the soul. Do not worry about this body and do your duty.

Hai Parth! According to the warrior code, you must wage war. It is a warrior's duty to fight evil. Today, evil stands before you fully armed.

It is your duty to fight it. If you die you will go to heaven. Get up, Arjuna and fight. Happiness / sorrow, gain / loss, victory / defeat are all the same. It is not only the code but also your duty.

Chapter 2,
Verse 37: Arise, resolve to fight:

Arjuna: My hands still refuse to pick up the Gandiva. I do not understand how I can justify this war. Do I benefit from it?

Krishna: Benefit? Loss? These are irrelevant. I know, you neither want heaven nor earth. Hence Arjuna! Go beyond victory / defeat, loss / gain, happiness / sorrow.

Arjuna: I still cannot move.

Krishna: Until now, I was appealing to your conscious mind which can discern right from wrong and recognise the voice of the soul. You are probably lost in its immortality. Weigh this moment in the balance of earthly action. Decide your duty from this aspect. You will arrive at the same conclusion that you must fight this war.

Arjuna: This is exactly what I cannot decide.

Krishna: You cannot make up your mind as you are conflicted with your emotions.

You are caught in the entanglement of attachments. Neither you nor humanity can benefit from your decision to not fight this war. Do not think of victory or defeat. Do your duty. Act!

Action is pure and meritorious. It is good for humanity. Action is its own reward. But if you act for your own good the action will be impure so, walk along the path of action for the greater good. The reward of your action is not in your control. So, act but do not expect any reward.

Lord is trying his best to persuade Arjuna on his role and duty, while Arjuna is bound by attachments, caught in the emotions, as this war is unlike any other war. The enemy is his family. If he wins the war, he loses as he will be killing his loved ones. Lord is inspiring and motivating Arjuna by explaining karma from which one cannot escape, the outcome of which is not in his hands, but to think why and what is the question.

Krishna: Dedicate your karma to the Lord and leave the result to the Lord. Is it not to uphold dharma? Is it not to prevent the growth of Adharma? Judge without misplaced compassion.

Verse 47 The yoga of knowledge:

Arjuna asks, how is an action without a motive or desire possible? Krishna! Reward motivates action. Without reward, who will act?

Krishna: Life is impossible without action. You may eat or not, you may give away food or not, you may wage a war or not, you have the option to do something or not do anything. The result is not in your hands. This action is the limit of your control. Even if you desire victory, it may not be yours, you could also lose the war.

Your desire to win will make you fear defeat. If you are indifferent to victory or defeat but fight the war as your duty, then there will be no question of happiness or sorrow. Such a desireless person is imperturbable. Hence, shed any desire for reward. Do what is within your control, which means, do your duty. This is Karma Yoga. Understand it well. You cannot control the result. You are an archer but if your target is not steady, you will miss it. You control your bow, arrow and your, but you cannot control the target. The true man does not cross the limits. Be steady and firm in your duty because its fulfilment is Yoga.

Arjuna asks: What is Yoga?

Krishna: Yoga is the fulfilment of duty, giving up temptations to do one's duty and the ability to be imperturbable.

**Chapter 2,
Verse 50: - Self-realisation**

Dhritarashtra: Sanjay!

Sanjay: Yes, my king.

Dhritarashtra: If Arjuna can hear you, tell him not to listen to Krishna. He is misleading Arjuna. Just think of it, Sanjay! Krishna came here as a peace messenger. Today he is not talking about peace, which means he did not want peace at all. He just wanted history to say that it was Dhritarashtra who did not want peace. Krishna has an agenda.

Sanjay says, "He is not talking of enmity; he is explaining the mystery of Truth and Karma Yoga."

Dhritarashtra: Now you are talking like him. Are you no longer loyal to me? Will you shift your loyalty?

Sanjay says, I am merely a narrator, my description has nothing to do with loyalty. I am doing my duty.

Dhritarashtra: Then do your duty as a narrator. Do not explain the meaning of Karma Yoga. Keep your eyes on them and tell me whatever is happening on the battlefield.

Dhritarashtra always worked in his self-interest. He never attempted to be a mediator and make peace between both sides to prevent the war from happening. He wanted his son to be the ruler. He was incapable of understanding the injustice done to Pandavas. How were they deceived in gambling and sent to live in forests? How Draupadi was humiliated and insulted in the courtyard? As a king he could not do justice to his own brother's sons to whom he was a guardian. His love for his sons clouded his judgement and sense of right and wrong. He was so selfish, unable to view and judge with his Jnana Netra. His attachment towards his son made him lose his balance of fairness with no respect to justice. He was so anxious to see his son Duryodhana win the war and rule the kingdom, while he was aware that the Lord was standing on the side of the Pandavas. When given a choice, Duryodhana chose the army over the Lord. How foolish was he?

Arjuna: How do I recognise an imperturbable man? What traits does he possess? How does he behave? How does he talk?

Krishna: It is not difficult to recognise such a man's rhetoric. Like him, you must shed your desires, free yourself from ambition. Go beyond happiness and sorrow. Neither happiness nor sorrow can change you. The imperturbable man always remains calm and balanced. He is undeterred. When he speaks, it is from the depth of his soul. He speaks not of attachment but of desireless action. (Nishkama Karma).

When he sits, he withdraws himself like a tortoise. He is his own fort. His senses are in his control. Only he who can control his senses can control his mind.

Chapter 2,
Verse 62/63: The source of Evil:

The ordinary mortal thinks of objects. This in turn leads to attachment, which leads to the birth of desires. When desires are unfulfilled it leads to anger, and anger gives birth to attachment. (Moha).

With this, the ability to think begins to stray. When this happens, intelligence is destroyed, this in turn leads to the downfall of the man. Temptations will impede and overshadow your intelligence. How can you get peace without intelligence? How can a person who cannot distinguish between peace and turmoil even be happy?

Arjuna! Like a gust of wind buffets the boat, desires dominate intelligence.

Chapter 2,
Verse 67: The means of deliverance:

Control your senses and do not let the senses control you. Listen to this with care and understand it. When the world sleeps, the enlightened man is awake. He only sleeps when the world awakes.

Arjuna: What does it mean to be awake when the world sleeps and sleep when the world is awake?

Krishna: I am not talking of night and day. I am talking of sleep and awakening. An ordinary / unwise man succumbs to temptations. This is the aim of awakening. He wants food when he is hungry. He wants water when he is thirsty. He needs a house for shelter. His thoughts are self-centred. The enlightened man's thoughts are selfless. He is beyond hunger, thirst, and he thinks of the greater good.

He does not think of the fallen fruit but the tree. An ordinary man needs fuel for his engine. The actions of this man are centred around his self-interest.

An intellectual man thinks of the importance of nature and the relationship of forests with nature and seasons. A materialistic man's day is the judicious man's night. The latter has none beyond duality. The materialistic man's night is the enlightened man's day. He awakens in the stillness of night.

**Chapter 2,
Verse 69:**

O' Arjuna! Truth is beyond senses. A philosopher is always in the quest for answers. A nonspiritual man's day is in the night. He is Sthitha Pragya.

A man who covets possessions is like a river that flows on eagerly without realising where it is going, only to squander its water into the sea. Even then the sea does not cross the limit of shore.

The river of desires overwhelms the craving man. However, a spiritual man can absorb it and still not cross the limit.

O' Arjuna! Become the sea of knowledge.

Chapter 3

Karma Yoga

Chapter 3, Verse 1:

Arjuna: O' Krishna! O' All knowing! If knowledge is essential, why are you asking me to do karma and fight the war when I have the knowledge of its outcome? These shifting thoughts bewilder me.

Why can't I walk away from fighting? My lord! Show me the path of welfare.

Arjuna is still in a state of not wanting to fight and has been asking many questions. This conversation is preordained and a wonderful opportunity to gain experience for the readers.

Karma is essential, but knowledge is superior. Executing the karma with knowledge through the mind is to be understood.

Chapter 3,
Verse 3: Self-development through action:

Arjuna! There are two types of people in the world. The meditator (Antar Mukhi) and the doers (Bahir Mukhi). The meditators search for God within themselves. He is a Jnana Yoga. The doers try to attain God through action, but there is no freedom from action. Searching for God within ourselves is also action.

So, Arjuna! There are only two paths: the path of Knowledge, (Jnana Yoga) path of Action, (Karma Yoga).

Arjuna asks, "Then why shouldn't I walk the path of knowledge?"

Lord says: Seeking knowledge does not mean giving up action, as life without action is impossible.

The man who forcibly suppresses the senses and tries to meditate is not Yogi. Yogi does not suppress the senses but controls them. He does not live with his eyes closed. The body's journey without action is impossible. Through the nose he will experience both fragrance and odour. Similarly, the ears will be exposed to euphony and cacophony.

The balanced man controls the senses and gives them direction with an awakened mind. He realises his options and knows how to organise them.

A human body gets the sight from the eyes, but a Yogi gets vision from the eyes. None of his senses are completely free. This separates the Yogi from an ordinary man. So, action is essential for salvation.

Chapter 3,
Verses 8 and 9 Spirit of self-dedicated activities:

Action should be like a Ritual (Yoga). Offering means any action should be performed with dedication and involvement. Action is a ritual, its aim being indestructible. The path of action goes straight to Avinashi Brahma (that cannot be destroyed). His life becomes less valuable if he does not participate in the life cycle. Do not go towards a life that has no value. The one whose actions and thoughts are self-centred is a sinner. Think of the greater good, recognise your duty and execute it.

Desire for a reward is the real obstacle. This is an impediment to progress. Society is not part of you, you are a part of society. Your prime duty is to the people's welfare. What is good for society is good for you.

Acting for the people's good is your salvation (siddhi); selfish action is a sin. It takes you away from the path of salvation.

Krishna: Remember Arjuna! You must achieve wonderful things. People who walk the path of desire and greed are not for greatness. People recognize and emulate the actions of other great men. " So, be a great man".

Chapter 3,
Verse 22: Resonate for Action:

Krishna: I do not need to do anything in the three worlds. There is nothing that I cannot obtain and yet, I am before you, doing my duty. I am doing Karma. I am proving to you that you can lead a life by performing an action and not expect any rewards in return.

Dhritarashtra was asking Sanjay: What is it that Krishna said? Sanjay replied that Krishna's voice changed at this point as if it were someone else that was speaking.

Dhritarashtra: Is there a third person?

Sanjay: I do not know what Arjuna understood, but no one, but the Lord can speak in such a tone. There is nothing that he cannot obtain. He said there was nothing worth doing, and yet he did not desist from action. If he did not act, the life cycle would stop, and humanity would cease to exist, and he would be responsible for it.

Dhritarashtra: No ordinary man can say this. Even a sage would not have the prowess to utter such words.

Sanjay: There was no pride in the manner Krishna delivered it.

Dhritarashtra: That is what makes me afraid. If he asked me to pick up a bow in such a tone, I would be oblivious to my impairment and do so. Sanjay! Will Arjun pick up the Gandiva?

Observe how Dhritarashtra is restless. He does not want Arjuna to succumb to Krishna's preaching. He worries that Arjuna would be ready for the war as Krishna preaches that it is for the good of humanity (Loka Kalyanam).

Sanjay: I cannot answer that question. If God wanted man to know the future, he would have given him the knowledge. So, let the future be born from the present. We can only wait.

Dhritarashtra: You are right. I know the result of war. Even so, I am hoping it would be different from what is going to happen. Until yesterday I thought, as a father of hundred sons, I will never be alone.

Continue to tell me about what is happening every moment at Kurukshetra.

Chapter 3, Verse 25:

Krishna: Arjuna! An ordinary man's actions are very self-centred. Yogi acts selflessly for the world and the welfare of the people. Dedicate your actions to me and fight the war. Death in the path of duty is welcome. In this path the demise of your teachers and elders will not be considered a sin.

Kartavya Palana Papa-Rahi tam. Kartavya Palan Kartrutva Bhavana: It is not a sin to execute one's responsibility. We are just instruments, and the divine force is doing it on our behalf.

If they die, their death will be for the good, if you die, your death will also be for the good. Therefore, fight; The path of truth cannot be the path of sin.

Arjuna: Talking of sin, why is a man compelled to sin? Who compels him?

Krishna: Lack of judgement. The path to choose right and wrong is always there. Choosing the wrong path compels him to sin. Recognise these enemies. Like the smoke covers the fire, dust cloaks the mirror. Desire, anger, lust cloak the knowledge.

Chapter 3, Verse 39:

The fire of temptation and desire is the enemy. So, Arjuna, get clarity and act accordingly.

**Chapter 3,
Verse 42: Scheme of Self-discovery:**

The power of the senses is no doubt great but greater than the senses is the mind. Greater than mind is reason (intellect) but the soul is the mightiest of all.

Partha! You are my disciple and my friend; hence I am, giving you this knowledge. In the beginning of creation, I preached to Surya who preached to Manu. Manu gave that wisdom to his son Ikshwak.

Arjuna: How is it possible, Partha? The Sun has existed for many years before you. How could you have given this knowledge to the Sun?

Science and Spirituality:

Human senses and mind: The soul is present in the body, which is the cause for all actions, when the body is said to be alive.

The moment the soul leaves the body; the body becomes inert, and it must be cremated.

The difference between life and death is the presence of the soul or Atman.

How do we recognise the soul? Soul is not an object or an organ; It can neither be seen nor felt through the touch.

We have five senses called Jnana Indriyas, five Karma Indriyas and a Mind.

Eye is Karma Indriya, vision is Jnana Indriya.

How do the eyes work in giving sight to a living body?

The reflecting ray from an object enters the eyes. A picture is made on the retina. It is carried to the brain. Yet there is no vision. Sensory nerves carry this impression Inwards to the nerve centre. The nerve centre in turn carries it to the brain. It is the brain's signals that lets us see the object / objects and it establishes vision.

Who is behind the brain / mind?

Let us take an object made of iron. When it is magnetised by passing the current through a wire that is wound around the iron piece, due to the induction of electromagnetic force, the iron piece attracts another object.

This is science. The force is invisible. The effect is neither seen nor felt.

Mind is present in all living beings. When the mind is inducted with the force of soul, it is activated and reacts to the impressions received from the centre, retina of the eye.

The state of Mind which reacts is known as Intellect. (Buddhi)

When and how does it react?

The soul is behind the mind, which is supreme and the 'Infinite Consciousness' that is 'Sat'.

Lord Krishna says, 'I am the Mind' that is activated.

In a human being, the soul is situated in the inner cave of the heart and is invisible to the eye. But its influence is felt through the entire body (like the sun rays falling on the entire universe).

This influence is felt as consciousness or awareness. The power to relish what we eat, the power of vision, power of touch and the auditory power is all on account of the soul.

The one who has an appetite to learn about the soul and understands it, is known as

'Atma Jnani' the seeker of knowledge on the self.

Accomplishment of Karma (Action):

For any creation four elements are required:

1. Para, 2. Pashyanti, 3. Madhyama, 4. Vaikhari

- A. When a thought to create something is conceived, it is called, 'Para'.

- B. The second stage would be to visualize and plan to execute the 'Para'. This is called Pashyanti.

- C. After moving to stage 3, gathering all the resources to execute the plan. This is known as Madhyama.

- D. When the plan goes into fruition, it is called Vaikhari.

One of the main preachings of Lord Krishna in Bhagavad Gita is to drive away the ego which is derived from obsessing about oneself where both the mind and buddhi are involved.

A person becomes happy / unhappy when his mind is happy / unhappy. There are two kinds of influences on the mind. One is external (family, friends, and colleagues) and the second one is internal through introspection. There could be positive and negative influences with internal and external influences. Our buddhi helps us deal with negative influences whether they are internal or external.

A person can walk properly when there is synchronisation between both legs.

For a person to be complete, there should be a symbiotic relationship between mind and Intellect. The integration of mind and buddhi makes the person singular.

Where there is a difference between the two, it makes the person dual.

It is exceedingly difficult to attain the state of singularity.

The Ego is the reason that stands for duality and the gap between mind and buddhi widens for an egotistical person.

The knowledge from the world around is acquired through the senses (Jnanedriyaas). The senses enable you to experience the world around you and evoke a reaction (spandana).

These reactions play a vital role which will determine singularity or duality. It dictates the mind and buddhi.

These reactions influence the Samskaras the person is carrying in both ways.

This will also lead to a conflict, resulting in the victory of the mind over Intellect or Intellect over mind and decide the destiny of the person for bad or good. The character and behaviour of the person is built on this.

Tattva Jnana says if the Samskaras a person carries are groomed in a right path then the negative influence on buddhi will be reduced.

If seen from a spiritual aspect, every person has an internal weapon i.e. buddhi. It can be used to drive away or clean the mind that has an accumulation of Samskaras. Most people do not use it or understand the importance of having good buddhi. They get entangled in the usual grind of life and are oblivious to the accumulation of bad Samskaras. If we are alive in this world, we need to constantly use the buddhi wisely. Can we leave the world or this body? By remaining in this world and with this body Gita advises to practice getting away from Moha (attraction, and attachment). This is where Arjuna failed in the battlefield. The weak buddhi will distort the mind that results in conflict and the senses lose their natural strength. The absorption of reality by buddhi will be hindered.

Gita says while performing the action (karma), one should put in the effort regardless of the outcome. This is Karma Yoga.

Chapter 4
Jnana Yoga

Verse 5; Theory of Incarnation:

Krishna: Arjuna, you and I have gone through many cycles of birth and death. I remember all those births, you don't. In a sense, I am eternal and indestructible, the Lord of all living beings (Jeeva's). The power that has been bestowed upon me has given birth to many incarnations.

Chapter 4, Verses 7 and 8:

> *Yada Yada Hi Dharmasya Glanir Bhavati Bharata*
> *Abhyutthanam Adharmasya Tadatmaanam Srujaamyaham*
> *Paritranaay Sadhunaam Vinashaya Cha Dushkritam*
> *Dharma Samsthapanarthaya Sambhavami Yuge Yuge*

I incarnate myself whenever truth is in danger, whenever evil threatens to take over, I come to protect the good and vanquish the evil. As a result, I have come to earth in many avatars.

Arjuna: But why does truth suffer?

Krishna: Justice suffers when a person in power cannot contain greed and temptation.

Krishna is playing all the events that took place that led them into the current state.

He reminded Arjuna how the house that they were living in, during their exile got burnt on the orders given by Duryodhana and the Pandavas were able to escape. He also reminded Arjuna about the egregious crime committed by the Kauravas on Draupadi. Krishna talked about the unspeakable atrocities committed by the Kauravas under the leadership of Duryodhana and how they did not deserve forgiveness,

Arjuna: Should I not be angry at Draupadi's disrobing?

Krishna: You must decide that. The disrobing of Draupadi in the presence of so many people is an unspeakable crime. If they cannot protect Draupadi, how can they provide protection to the ordinary women in their kingdom?

Hence, disrobing is a greater societal issue. It is your duty to identify those who dared to disrobe Draupadi. They are the enemies of society. Do not hesitate to fight with all those men who side with Evil.

Here Krishna makes Arjuna recollect the past events and inspires him to analyse the good and evil. Krishna was very methodical in making Arjuna understand that Bhishma, the sage Drona, the teacher who was all silent, when the incident of disrobing was happening in the presence of people is a cowardly act for men of that stature. Krishna was trying hard to explain to Arjuna that justice should prevail even if he must pay a price for sacrificing his relationships with his loved ones. Krishna is pulling Arjuna out from Moha and tries to make him aware of his duty.

Rise above personal anger and fight for the people (Loka Kalyanam).

This is your prime duty (Kartavya Palana Kartrutva Bhavana).

Look at me. I did create this society but do not desire a reward for it. Though I am the creator I am beyond it. The man who sees the truth finds freedom.

Chapter 4, Verse 14:

I desire no reward, so my action is selfless. Act without desire and greed. Distinguish between action, inaction, and bad action. (Karma, Akarma, Vikrama)

Arjuna: What is the difference between these?

Action when performed should be free from desire. Inaction is neither good for society nor for oneself. Bad action is harmful to society and to oneself. The doer is superior to the non-doer (Karta - Akarta) as Action is superior to Inaction (Karma- Vikrama).

Non-doers do not deserve rewards. Doer is a selfless person. The action itself is the reward for the doer. He moves to the next action without expecting / receiving a reward. The doer is motivated by the result for the greater good.

Thus, when a non-doer becomes a doer, he merely does what is essential for life. All other actions are good for society, his very existence is good for society. Such a life is a ritual offering to God. You too must make such an offering. Burn down all desires, greed, and anger.

Arjuna: What is yagna - the ritual of offering?

Krishna: It has several meanings. For some, it is the Supreme God (Brahma Swaroopa). For some, it is meant to please God, and for others it is the soul unification with God.

Likewise, there are various kinds of offerings. Some offer wealth or material things, while others offer services.

There are four types of offerings:

1. Wealth - Dravya Yajna – wealth is used for the good of society.

2. Tapo Yajna - When a person makes his actions his penance, his life becomes Tapo Yagna. Doing your duty is also Yagna. It benefits the person as well as humanity.

3. Yoga Yajna - Yoga is studied as a subset of this. It takes the person to meditation.

4. Jnana Yajna - All four are important but Jnana Yagna is the most important, because proper use of knowledge can distinguish between good and bad. The fire of knowledge can purify action. Knowledge is the focus of the essence of Action. Knowledge frees you from the bonds of temptations. Only knowledge can cross the sea of sin.

Karma is inevitable even to God. Performing Karma is also Dharma. God cannot even change Karma. It must be accepted.

An animal does not harm its own species, but a human being does. A person is always carrying either dharma or adharma. This is not an object but a Samskara.

Krishna says dharma can prevail if this war is fought. Dharma brings courage, energy, and Intelligence.

Birth and death are the result of Karma. Karma is the cause for happiness or sorrow. One needs to accept the Karma and pray to God for courage and wisdom to live a truthful life.

When Karma is performed with understanding and realisation, it paves the way for salvation, in the absence of which life will be binding. One needs to be self-aware in performing the action. The Karma Yogi offers the Karma itself to God.

There is truth behind everything, every matter. If you are on the seashore, you notice the ebb and flow of the waves that are filled with foam. The foam gives an illusion that there is something in the water, but it is just water. This realization comes from Jnana.

So, you and I are not real but the Atman within us is real which makes us think and act to perform the Karmas.

Our every action should become a prayer with dedication by which one becomes God. Nothing in this creation can satisfy you. Only acquiring knowledge will give you eternal satisfaction.

One must prepare himself before departing from this life. One must complete their responsibility before that. The quintessence of life is procreation. Every species that comes into this world procreates. When one procreates, it is imperative that the progeny is given all the 'Samskaras' to lead a worthy life. Thus, the legacy continues.

One should be like Lord Krishna on the battlefield who was not fighting, but directing with guidance and inspiring his followers?

Chapter 5

Karma Sannyasa Yoga

Arjuna is asking Bhagwan:

Krishna! You talk about Karma Sannyasa (dejecting the action) and Karma Yoga. Which one should I follow? Which is superior?
Lord replied, Arjuna! Both are necessary, but of these two, Karma Yoga is superior to Karma Sannyasa. One who has renounced worldly pleasures, because he is beyond the duals of like - dislike, can easily be freed from all attachments of the world.

Because one who adopts and follows Karma Yoga and Karma Sannyasa will attain the Lord.

Jnana Yogis who attain the path of liberation can also attain it by Karma Yoga. One who sees both Yogas as one has reached the pinnacle of Jnana.

Arjuna! Without understanding Karma Yoga, it is difficult to renounce the actions performed by mind, senses, and the body.

Arjuna asked Krishna to explain the attributes of a Yogi.

Krishna: One, whose mind is under control and who wins over the senses, has a purified conscience, and sees his soul in all beings which is the real form of Lord, will never be binding.

By offering all actions, executing the actions with no expectations is like a drop of water on a lotus leaf. Water drops slide on the leaf and does not get absorbed by the leaf.

Similarly, the philosopher Yogi is not attached to the action and its results. Yogi performs actions with no intention of desire and expectations.

The nishkama-karma Yogi remains at peace as he depicts the results of Karma. One who performs action with expectations/desires always lives the life of anticipation. Happiness is a state of mind that can be attained by being conscientious in doing the Karma and expecting nothing in return. The Lord is not the shareholder of any sin or virtue of a person.

When the Jnana is covered with the Ajnana of a person, he / she fails to see things clearly. However, Ajnana vanishes with Jnana attained from Lord. Jnana shines like the Sun in the sky.

One will be liberated from the cycle of birth / death with constant meditation and Jnana practice. Thus, the soul attains Brahma.

A sinless person who frees himself from all doubts and desires the wellness of all beings, remains with the Lord in his meditation.

He wins over anger, desire and sees the Lord all over. He never allows his mind to think of the external world but focuses on the 'Jnana Chakshu' located on the forehead in between the eyebrows and maintains a rhythm even while breathing.

In this process, mind, intellect and senses will be surrendered to practitioners. From their practice, Yogis will be liberated.

Lord is the beneficiary from yajna and penance, who is the chief administrator to all worlds.

A Jnani who knows the Lord is pleased with all beings and gets eternal peace.

The person is the traveler in the body chariot. Intellect is the chariot driver. Mind is the instrument that drives. Senses are horses. Sense objects are the paths. Thus, the soul is beneficiary of Mind & Senses.

Chapter 6

Dhyana Yoga

Bhagwan said, a person that performs his / her duty with no expectations is the real sanyasi. God is flawless and looks after every being equally. Jnanis are beyond the three Gunas (three attributes) and are liberated beings. One who is impervious to losses and gains, one who is always stable, one who does not succumb to material possessions is known as Brahma. He is extremely focused and practices meditation to achieve equanimity.

What is real happiness?

The pleasures derived from the senses are momentary and fleeting. They have a beginning and an end. A person who seeks spiritual knowledge is not affected by the material world. One who controls and manages anger, desires and stress is a real practitioner and can become a Yogi.

Arjuna! The so-called sanyasi is also known as Yogi. Unless the 'will' is renounced, one cannot become a Yogi.

Which Yogi is superior?

For the Yogi practitioner, action is an instrument. A successful Yogi can practice sannyasa.

A Yogi gives up worldly pleasures and leads a life in the quest of spiritual knowledge.

A Yogi is incredibly happy in his own company.

Resisting temptations of material things is quintessence of the life of a Yogi.

A Yogi does not get impacted by external forces. A Yogi is impervious to insults / accolades and happiness / grief. A Yogi is above all these emotions. He has a single-minded devotion to God and practices Yogic life for the Atman to be one with God.

How to meditate?

Create a setting conducive to meditation by sitting in a straight posture, aligning the head, back, neck and by controlling the senses and mind with a focus on consciousness. Keep your focus on the tip of your nose. It takes a lot of practice to attain the meditative state. Bringing the mind under control and with steady focus on the Lord, one can develop and gain mastery in this practice.

When the meditative practice culminates, one can experience equanimity. This state of super happiness comes from feeling liberated from the worldly pleasures.

Krishna: A Yogi offers his prayers to me, sees me in everybody and everything. I reside within such a Yogi.

Arjuna! A person who treats everyone equally and perceives grief and happiness as the same is a superior being.

What is Mind?

How is it possible to control the mind?

Arjuna asks Lord Krishna,

O Madhusudana! How can I calm my wavering mind? I am unable to cajole it. I am unable to be objective and determine whether doing what is needed to restore Dharma is more important than restoring relationships.

Krishna: Kaunteya! The mind is very fickle, and it is exceedingly difficult to control it. However, a lot can be achieved with a proper frame of mind and practice. One who is unsuccessful in controlling the mind cannot be qualified to become a Yogi.

It is my strong opinion that it is possible with constant practice.

What happens to people that leave this world before they attain equanimity? What happens to their soul? Have they left this world as a lost soul?

The deeds of this lifetime will determine the good karma or bad karma a person accrues. Not attaining the Yogic state will never be viewed by God as a bad virtue.

A Yogi takes all the fruits of the virtuous deeds and the Yogic practice to his / her next life.

Yogi is supreme of all i.e. Tapasvi. So, you become a Yogi.

Of all Yogis, one who meditates with consciousness with devotion is supreme to me. **How does a mantra work?**

Mantras are powerful vibrations.

So, to create powerful vibrations, chanting of mantras is the best practice. The word mantra means **'mananat trayate iti mantra'** which says, 'you are protected because of the powerful vibrations that were created'.

Mantras attract divine forces by which one overcomes obstacles in life. If there is a law of gravity, there must be a law of grace. By the power of grace, obstacles in life have been mysteriously solved and that is the grace of the Lord. By chanting a mantra, you invoke the process in a mysterious dimension. God helps us in his own way, but we must be cognizant of God's grace.

By chanting mantra, you create magnetic force, wherein such a divine hand will allow us mysteriously to help us in our daily lives.

As Paramaatma Lord Krishna dwells in all bodies, knows about the bodies and their Actions. Though Atma and Paramaatma are one and same, realizing the difference among the two is the Wisdom. It is like water in a vessel taken out from ocean, water in mighty ocean. Both waters are the same and one.

Mantra is a Good Energiser. Let mantra chanting be an everyday ritual to seek the grace of the Lord.

Jeeva and Deva:

When a person is aligned with the world / nature he becomes Jeeva.

If the same person is in the quest for knowledge of understanding that 'Tat' which casts its influence on the entire body, senses, organs etc. and detaches from the world and develops attachment with that 'Tat', he becomes a Deva.

Bhakti is realised in the form of love itself. One must see the loving form of God in everything. This is the basis of Bhakti.

How is it possible?

Realisation of love comes when one's actions towards a person are altruistic and devoid of expectations. In the final stage, consciousness of one's own body does not exist.

In the case of Jnani, he realises the oneness everywhere and sees himself as the self in everything without any ego (Aham).

Vedanta says Brahman as "Sat Chit Ananda"

It means:

Sat - existence

Chit - consciousness or knowledge

Anand - bliss or love

Both Bhakta and Jnani have no difference on 'Sath'.

Jnani lays greater stress on 'Chit' or knowledge, while Bhakta keeps the aspect of Ananda or love more in view.

The understanding and realization of the essence of 'Chit' leads to the realization of 'Ananda'.

Chapter 7
Jnana VIjnana Yoga

Arjuna! Surrender to me – unparallel surrender and devotion to me alone. I will teach you about yoga practice and how you will start to understand me. You would have conquered the understanding of most things once you know 'Tattva Jnana'.

How to know the Lord?

There are very few people in this world who understand me.

Nature is with eight elements earth, water, fire, air, space, mind, intellect, and ego. It is known as 'Apara Prakruti'.

Different from this is 'Para Prakruti' which bears the life-based universe.

All living things on this planet start their journey from 'Apara Prakriti' and 'Para Prakriti'.

The creation in the universe starts with me and ends with me. I am the anchor of the universe.

I am everywhere. I am the fire in the sun, light in the moon, sound in space, fragrance in a flower, life in all lives and I am the penance. I am the desire that exemplifies dharma.

Partha! I am the eternal seed to all beings. I am the intellect and the strength in people.

I created this world, and it is all 'Maya'. You can see 'Sattva, Rajas and Tamas' in all humans, but I am beyond those attributes.

Types of devotees:

My illusion is with three Gunas. It is impossible to go beyond these three Gunas. One can be free from the illusion who surrenders to me and meditate all the time.

Those who are entangled with illusion are ignorant. People that exude satanic traits do not offer their prayers to me.

O Bharat! Devotees are classified in four categories.

Those who desire wealth and pleasure.

Those who are in distress.

Those who desire to reach God

Those who are Jnani

Those who meditate on me constantly with no diversion to the external world are Jnanis and I feel very close to these people. Jnanis bear my form (Swaroopa) and such devotees surrender to me by keeping their minds and intellects on me. After multiple births, Jnani feels Vasudeva is omnipresent.

Sakama / Nishkama:

Sakama devotees are those who offer prayers to the gods / deities to fulfil their desires. Nishkama devotees are those that are impervious to the result of their prayers. They have no expectations or desires.

My devotees have a deep understanding of who I am. There are those that are enveloped in ignorance. They are unable to see that I am not ordinary. I am engulfed in yoga maya and cannot be seen by all. Jnanis can understand me and know that I am eternal.

Arjuna! I know everything that has happened in the past or has happened in the present or going to happen in the future and about all beings.

The people that free themselves from the entanglement of life and are virtuous in their actions can eradicate their sins. Such people become free from duals and will understand Paramatma.

Chapter 8

Akshara Brahma Yoga

What are Adibhutam, Aadidaivam and Adiyagya?

Arjuna asked, O Purushottama! What is Brahma? What is Adhyatma? What is Karma? What is Aadi Bhutam, Aadi Daivam and Aadi Yagam? How does the Aadi Yagam appear in this body?

Lord replied:

The supreme, eternal is known as Brahma. Adhyatma talks about Jeevaatma.

Karma, whether good or bad causes birth and death. The body is temporary in this world. It appears with the birth and vanishes with the death. The soul remains forever and that is called Aadi Bhutam.

Hiranyagarbha is the Aadidaivam, who created this universe through Brahma.

Arjuna! I am known as Adiyagya when I live in everyone's heart as Antaryaami.

O' Kounteya!

Every human that comes into this world must leave. Those are the laws of nature. The actions of that lifetime determine whether that human will be born again.

Keep me in your thoughts. With undeterred focus of the mind, meditate on my form. This will help you reach the divine Purusha Paramatma.

How can one get close to the lord?

The centre point between the eyebrows is called 'Bhrukuti'. Focus your mind by fixing it on the 'Bhrukuti.

The Vedic Scholars describe that a 'Sanyasi' adopts Brahmacharya to attain Para Brahman.

Partha! One who attains Siddhi known as Mahatma reaches me and they will fall into the cycle of birth and death.

How is the age of Brahma decided?

A thousand yuga is one day and equal to one night for Brahma. He created the universe in one day.

Though all lives end, the abode of the Lord remains. All lives merge with the Lord. The Lord who is omnipresent and occupies the entire universe, will be obtained through single minded devotion / meditation.

There are two ways of leaving the world:

One is called Devyana and the other is called Pitruyana.

The Brahma scholars reach the abode of the Lord and remain in Brahma Pada. The divine deities take them during the period of Sukla fortnight, in Uttaraayanam. A year is made in two parts. Uttaraayanam is the journey of the Sun towards North, six months period from December to June. While the journey of the Sun towards the south Is called Dakshinaayanam which is from June to December.

Uttaraayanam is daytime for Devatas, Dakshinaayanam is night-time for Devatas known as Krishna fortnight.

Some of us take the Devayana route, liberated from this world and never come back. There are those who will take the Pitruyana route that will leave this world and come back with a rebirth.

Chapter 9

Raja Vidya Raja Guhya Yoga

O' Arjuna! You are a virtuous man. I will teach you the most sacred knowledge. Once you master it, you will become free from the entanglement with this Samsara.

One who has no trust and devotion revolves in the cycle of birth and death.

I am omnipresent. Everything that happens in this universe is as per my order. At the end of the creation, all beings will merge with me.

Again, in the beginning of creation I will create them. All these are under my influence of nature (Prakruti); they are not independent. Nature is within my control.

How to serve God?

<u>Krishna:</u> I am the yajna, I am the medicine, I am the mantra, I am the fire. I am the homam (Ritual performed by offering prayers through the fire to please the deities). I am the father, mother, and the protector of the universe.

I am the Omkar; I am the Vedas and the destination-Parama dharma.

I am a bearer, friend and cause for the creation and destruction. I am the refuge for devotees. I am the Sun to convert the sea into clouds with rain to shower. I am the nectar. I am 'Sat' (eternal soul). I am also 'A-Sat', the material that will not last long.

Those who meditate and pray to other deities are my devotees too. In the end, no matter who they pray to, I am the object for all yajnas. They are not recognising the Tattva, the philosophy of Paramaatma. That is why they descend. Those who meditate deities (devatas) reach Devloka and those who meditate ancestors reach Pitruloka.

Can the people that have sinned attain the lord?

Krishna: I treat all beings equally. One who is totally devoted to me resides within me.

Those that have committed sins seek redemption by chanting my name and meditate with their focus on me and surrender to me.

Chapter 10

Vibhuti Yoga

How is the divine Tattva?

Krishna: Arjuna, your love, and devotion for me is unrivalled, and I feel compelled to repeat my teachings so that you can find an answer to the conflict in your mind.

Nobody knows my powers in this world. This includes the mighty rishis and deities. They do not know that they exist because of me.

A Jnani understands the reason for my existence. Such a person believes in me unconditionally and attains 'Moksha'.

The qualities such as intellect, empathy, honour, control of senses, happiness, sorrow, birth, destruction, fear, courage, peace, equality, penance, charity, recognition, reproach are all being experienced because of me.

The Saptha Rishis and their predecessors, Sanaka Sadananda Munis were all my devotees. They all are born out of my will. All humans are the descendants of those Rishis.

The magnificent divine excellence if understood by anyone will know that I am the origin and cause for this creation. The universe functions because of me. People who know this serve me forever with utmost faith. Their mind and prana remain with me. They always talk about me. They enjoy being with me. They keep their mind on me and serve me with love. I present them with the Buddhi Yoga.

Arjuna: Krishna, you are Parabrahma, Parama-Dharma and the purest of all. You are divine, an ancient god with no rebirth and omnipresent. You are spoken very highly of by Rishis such as Veda Vyasa and Narada.

O' Keshava! Whatever you said is true. Hey! Bhagwan! Even Devatas or Daanavaas cannot perceive your real form.

O' Purushottam! Bhautesh! Deva! Your philosophy is supreme. You have occupied all the worlds with your divine attributes. You are the manifestation of those attributes.

O' Yogeshwar! Please guide me on how I can meditate. How can I focus without any distraction?

O' Janardhana! Please tell me about your yoga power, and the glories of your divine attributes. You totally mesmerized me, and I am grateful to you for whatever I have imbibed with all your teachings and yet I feel that I have so much to learn. Even with your profound teaching, I am still not convinced.

Krishna: Arjuna! You said wisely. There is no end to my divine attributes but allow me to explain.

I remain in the hearts of all beings as Atman. I am the beginning, middle and end of all beings. I am one of the twelve sons of Aditya, as Vishnu. I am the Sun's rays. I am Marichi among the forty-nine Vayu Deities. I am the Sun among stars. I am the Samaveda among the Vedas. I am Indra among the Devatas. I am the mind among senses. I am the conscious among the beings.

I am Shankar among Rudraas. I am Kubera among Yakshas. Among Vasus I am Agni (fire). I am the Meru among mountains. I am Brihaspati among the priests.

In water bodies I am the Ocean. Among Rishis, I am Bhrigu. I am Omkar, one syllable among sounds. Among all Yajnas, I am Japa Yajna. In stable objects, I am Himalaya. I am Aswath tree among trees, Narada among Deva Rishis. I am Chitrarath from Gandhar, Kapila Maharshi among Siddhas. Among horses, I am Uchchaihshrava, who evolved from the milky ocean along with the nectar, Aira vat, among elephants. I am the king among the people, Vajra among weapons. I am Kamadhenu among cows.

I am Manmatha of love, Vasuki among Snakes, Ananta among Nagas. Of all water deities I am Varun. Among my ancestors I am Aryama. Yama Dharmaraja among dictators, Prahlad among demons, Lion among animals, Garuda among birds, Vaayu among those that purify. Rama among soldiers, Crocodile in the water, river Ganga among rivers. I am the beginning and end of creation. I am the supreme knowledge among all knowledge, I am the alphabet in the language. I am Time. I am Viraat Purusha with the form of the Universe. I am the bearer and nourisher. I am a productive stint among beings. I am the glory, wealth, speech, memory, intelligence and forgiveness.

In music I am Brihastamam among all shrutis (tunes). I am the brilliance in a mind, victory among winners. I am Satva Guna among Satvik people. Vasudeva among Yadavas. Arjuna among the Pandavas, Vyasa among Munis. Shukracharya among poets. I am the punishment who awards / executes punishment. I am morality in those who desire victory.

I am the answer to the mystery. In Jnanis, I am that knowledge of philosophy i.e. Tattva means who is universal and who controls. I am the seed for the creation of beings.

In this universe there is stability and instability, but nothing is without me.

O seeker of truth! There is no end to my attributes. The extent of which I have explained to you. Anything that has glory, radiance, power is from my brilliance.

Chapter 11

Vishwaroopa Darshana Yoga

Arjuna requested the lord to show him the Vishwarupa.

O' Krishna! Your preaching has unravelled the secret of spirituality. I feel liberated from delusion (Moha). I have imbibed your teachings and learned so much about the creation and destruction of the universe. Your eternal greatness glows with splendour. You have spoken the ultimate truth that can never be repudiated.

O' Lord! I am longing to see your divine form. Please show me the eternal form.

Krishna: Arjuna! Innumerable forms will appear in my divine form when you see them. Adityas, Vesuvius, Rudraas and Ashwini deities will appear. My body and mind in its entirety is the universe. You need divine vision to witness and withstand my Vishwarupa and my yoga shakti.

How is Vishwarupa? Dhritarashtra asked Sanjaya.

O'King! Lord Krishna showed his divine form to Arjuna. In those infinite faces and innumerable eyes appeared. The divine form is filled with ornaments, garlands, silk fabric covering the body and the arms holding many weapons. The sandalwood fragrance has engulfed the air around. His many forms create wonder and bliss. It emanates the light of a thousand suns. Arjuna saw innumerable worlds in that form in one place and the spectacle was indefinable. Arjuna folded his hands and bowed to Krishna with utmost devotion.

Arjuna: O'Deva! I am seeing all deities. Brahma seated on a lotus, Shankara, all Rishis, divine snakes on your body. Your form is illuminated. I am not finding your beginning and end. You look magnificent and are shining like the radiating sun. You are indestructible Para-brahma and hence knowable. You are the main cause for this universe and the eternal protector and ancient purusha.

The wide span of your shoulders, the eyes that are like the sun and the moon, the face like a burning fire, the radiation from your body becomes the object of meditation to all. I am seeing your magnificent form and there is a dearth of words to explain the indescribable feeling.

Mahatma! You have occupied the entire space from earth to sky and are shining in all directions. Your form appears wonderful, you are revered by many, and your power is feared by those that inflict suffering on others. All deities are chanting your name with folded hands. Maharishis, Siddhis are reciting Stotra's in their prayers.

Rudra's, Adityas, Vesuvius, Sadhus, Vishwa devatas, Ashwini devatas, ancestors, Yakshas, demons are all watching you in wonder. I cannot seem to come out of this admiration and amazement, and I also fear your power. On seeing this formidable form of yours, I must confess that I am terrified of your immense power.

O my Lord! Please bestow upon me the courage and your grace. I am seeing the sins of the Kauravas.

The locusts got attracted to the fire and burned themselves. Similarly, all these people are reaching a point of no return. They may not fathom your power and as a result cannot understand the consequences of following Adharma.

O Lord Vishnu! All these worlds are contained in you. You are the protector of good and punisher of evil.

Please enlighten me on your fearful form as I have not witnessed a form with such fury. I am eager to understand the ancestral god.

Krishna: Arjuna! I am the Kaal (Time) to finish all worlds. Even if you do not fight the war, you cannot save the lives of the people who are fighting for your enemy. Their life and death are deterministic. So, fight and win the war. Victory will be yours and you will be remembered for your prowess in the battlefield and the protector of Dharma. You will be remembered for eternity. You can rule the kingdom and provide prosperity to the people.

Have no fear my friend. You are merely an instrument in this whole endeavour. The deaths of Bhishma, Drona, Karna and others are preordained. The war is a medium and you are just a tool.

On listening to the words of Krishna, Arjuna was overwhelmed and struggled to utter the words.

Arjuna: O' Rishikesh! The entire world revels in your glory. The demons understand your wrath and are fearful of antagonizing you. The saints are praying for you. You are the supreme. You are the prime subject before Brahma. You are the form of syllables. You are the ancient purusha. You are the asylum for the entire universe. The entire universe is within you. You are the Vaayu, (AIR), Yama, fire, Varuna, moon. You are the father to Brahma. I offer thousands of prayers to you.

You represent infinite strength. I pray to you in every form. You are my friend, Yadava, Sakha, Krishna. You are the father, teacher, Pujya, and deva of this universe. There is no one mightier than you.

Hence, I submit myself to you and I plead with you to forgive me for my ignorance in understanding who you really are.

Please come back from your Vishwarupa to your original form and bless me.

Krishna: Arjuna! My Viswarupa is radiant and infinite. You are my ardent devotee, and you have earned this gift to see the Virat form with my yoga shakti. I have not given this privilege to anyone other than you. There are many accomplished yogis and rishis in this world who have never experienced what you have with my Vishwarupa. I bestowed upon you this enormous wealth of knowledge. I have faith that you will walk the righteous path. Now I will return to my original form.

Arjuna: Janardhana! Now I am at peace in seeing you in human form. My mind feels like a tranquil place.

Krishna: You have seen my divine form. You are the only one that can see me in that form and understand the meaning of my incarnation. Many deities are eager to see this form and learn about my divine form. That is only possible for those with a single-minded devotion to me.

Chapter 12

Bhakti Yoga

Meditation and Idol Worship:

Arjuna: O Krishna! Some devotees meditate while others do idol worship. Is one better than the other?

Krishna: Arjuna! By focusing your mind on me and thinking about me incessantly, offering prayers to me will make you a supreme Yogi.

Yogis are those who bring their senses under their control and look at all life forms as the same. They are beyond the Mind and the Intellect.

Jnana is supreme to practice (Sadhana).

Meditation is superior to Jnana, sacrificing the benefits of karma is still superior to meditation.

One attains peace by sacrifice.

Who can attain the Lord?

One who has no animosity towards anyone, one who has kindness and compassion, one who has no ego, one who doesn't get overjoyed in victory and perturbed in defeat, one who has control over the mind, who is determined and who offers their mind and Jnana to me and one who is just.

One who does not harm others, one who cannot be instigated by others, one who is not envious of others, one who is fearless gets my attention and blessings. One who sacrifices for the greater good has a special place in my heart.

Chapter 13
Kshetra Kshetrajna Vibhaga Yoga

Lord explains to Arjuna about Jnana.

This body is known as Kshetram. One who knows about Kshetram is Kshetrajna, which means Jeevaatma. Jnana means the knowledge of knowing Kshetra and Kshetrajna are related to the body and the soul.

What is Kshetra? Who is a Kshetrajna? These are explained by the Rishis in several ways. Vedas have their own interpretation as well.

Scientifically it is decided in Brahma sutras.

In brief, the body is composed of five elements (Earth, Air, Fire, Water and Ether) ego.

Jnana is an important part of human evolution. To learn is to acquire knowledge. Using knowledge wisely requires wisdom. Jnana is wisdom. If you acquire Jnana, it helps the mind to discern good from bad, right from wrong.

Who is God? Where is He?

God is omnipresent. He has occupied every corner in the universe. He rules the entire world. He is formless. He lives in all life forms. He is everywhere and nowhere. He is far but also close. He is like the sky, un-divisible. He is a creator like Brahma, sustainer like Vishnu, and a destroyer like Rudra.

He is the light and beyond darkness. He is the form of knowledge and destination for knowledge. He lives in the hearts of everybody. One who recognises this will reach me.

Why do rebirths happen?

Nature (Prakriti) and Purusha have no beginning. The three Gunas (Sattva, Rajas, Tamas) are born from nature.

The cause and effect are a product of nature. The Jeeva-Atman enables you to experience pain and pleasure. Purusha by being in Nature, experiences the attributes developed from nature.

How can one be liberated from the cycle of birth and death:

The Ataman (soul) is really Paramatma. He is called the presider, consort, beneficiary, and Maheshwara. The one who understands the forms of nature and purusha, performs all the karmas and will not undergo the cycle of birth and death.

Some people meditate via the soul (Atman) through Dhyana Yoga in their heart. Some, through Karma Yoga or Jnana Yoga have darshan of the soul.

Arjuna! Know that the birth of a person is caused by the meeting of the Kshetra and Kshetrajna. Bodies are perishable but Eswara is non-destructive. The one who sees the divine soul is the one with the vision. One who sees the Eeshwar in everything and everybody, reaches the abode of the Lord.

All actions (Karmas) have happened through nature (Prakriti). One who knows that the soul is not the subject in performing the action can see the truth. All of us have one Atman. It is important to understand that there is only the same Atman in all of us. Recognizing and understanding this is becoming Brahma.

Atman is immortal, non-destructive and not the subject of any karma. Though the soul is present in the body (being) it cannot carry the attributes.

As the sun shines in the entire universe, so does the soul shine in all life forms. Thus, one who knows the difference between Kshetra and Kshetrajna and one who understands the path to liberation from nature through wisdom will attain the abode.

As Paramaatma Lord Krishna dwells in all bodies, knows about the bodies and their Actions. Though Atma and Paramaatma are one and same the two is the Wisdom. It is like water in a vessel taken out from the ocean, water in a mighty ocean. Both waters are the same and one.

Chapter 14

Guna Traya Vibhaga Yoga

Krishna: All rishis in supreme state with supreme knowledge and practice will be able to attain me. They will be liberated from the cycle of birth and death.

Reason for Rebirth:

I am the seed in the womb, which is the form of Brahma, the origin of nature, the birthplace for all beings.

The origin of Nature (Moola Prakruti) is the mother of all beings. I am the father to establish the seed for all these beings.

How do the attributes bind the person?

The attributes born from nature (Sattva, Rajas, Tamas) bind the eternal soul in the body. Of these three, Sattva is the purest form, one that radiates and has no disorder / distortion. It makes the soul bind with happiness and wisdom.

Rajas are the attributes for desires and lust and bind the soul with action.

Tamas is born from Ignorance. It shields the Jnana (Wisdom).

How does each attribute influence?

Sattva is developed in the body in which consciousness is activated with knowledge through the nine open channels in the body.

When Rajas are not controlled, the attributes such as desires, greed and lust will not be tamed, and it makes it hard to attain the yogic state.

In the case of Tamas, it dulls the consciousness, does not fulfill the karmic actions that are supposed to be, and exhibits complacency.

In the case Sattva is developed, the virtuous one who leaves the body reaches the sacred world.

In the case of Rajas, rebirth is inevitable as the one that leaves the body is attached to the actions (Karma).

In the case of Tamas, death of a human results in the rebirth of a life form that is not human.

Actions with virtues will lead to the fruits of Sattva, actions with Rajas will lead to rebirth with grief, actions with Tamas will lead to ignorance.

Sattva is superior in nature and will lead to higher worlds, the Rajasic attribute will lead to human worlds and the Tamas will lead to the underworld.

Those who are above the three attributes can understand the philosophy of the divine and reach the lord. They will be liberated from the cycle of birth and death and attain divinity.

Arjuna asked Krishna, "How can I recognize the person who is beyond all the three attributes? How does this person function? How does he manage the attributes of nature?"

Lord Replied, "One who goes beyond the three attributes is starved for knowledge and abnegates the worldly desires. This person would have attained a spiritual state. He is not influenced by the external factors and remains forever in Atman. He treats the duality equally, such as grief / happiness and victory / loss. He is apathetic to material things. He never gets agitated in any situation. He is apathetic to accolades / insults, pleasure / pain, and likes / dislikes. The one who performs the action with devotion, without attachment, and no expectation is known as Trinitarian. He who meditates with Bhakti Yoga and is a Trinitarian can attain the state of Brahma. I am the foundation for attaining eternal Brahma, divinity, eternal set of duties and infinite happiness.

Chapter 15

Purushottama Yoga

How to understand the Philosophy of the lord?

Lord Krishna talks about the tree that is compared to Samsara (worldly life). The quintessential part of the tree is its roots, and all the roots are underground and not visible.

The cosmic tree is represented as a huge, inverted tree and is known as tree of life or upside-down tree. It symbolizes the entire universe. The roots are in the sky and the energy and wisdom is dispensed to earth through the branches. This tree connects heaven, earth, and the underworld. In reality, the inverted tree is maya. The reflection of a tree on the bank in the water describes an inverted tree. It is ignorance when one forgets the true source is roots and leaves and branches cease to exist without the roots.

The branches are developed with the attributes of Sattva, Rajas and Tapas.

The branches that grow hang down and spread. Tender leaves are the worldly pleasures that grow and spread. In this world, the roots of the tree of Samsara grow stronger and spread due to the bond with the worldly pleasures.

A tree truly symbolizes altruism. It provides food and shelter to so many life forms. However, when the tree dies and falls to the ground on our path, it is a mere inconvenience. We should lead virtuous lives like the tree and make ourselves beneficial to society. When we fall off the righteous path, we are just like a dead tree and are just a burden to everyone around us.

One who recognizes and understands the concept of an inverted tree has attained Paramaatma Tatvam (Philosophy of Lord).

Since time is immortal, and the entire universe evolved, developed and spread all over, one must surrender to him. One who wins over ego, attachment and passion will understand the eternal philosophy and become a Jnani and reach the abode of the Lord. The self-effulgence of my abode cannot be illuminated by either sun, moon or fire. Those who reach the abode will never return to this world in any form.

How can one find the soul entering another body? The way the wind carries the fragrance, the Jeevaatma, while leaving the body carries the mind and senses and enters another body. It attains a form with the mind and other organs to function.

There are those that are enveloped in ignorance and cannot recognise this. However, a Jnani uses the wisdom through (Jnana Netra) will know this science.

Those who practice spirituality and live with the soul constantly, become yogis. Those who have not cultivated good thoughts and consciousness cannot find the soul despite their efforts.

Where does the lord reside in the human body?

The brightness of the moon and the radiation from the sun are generated by me. I enter the earth with my energy, I bear all forms of life, and I provide nourishment. I am present in all life forms as "Jhataraagni" and allow the food to digest.

I am known through the Vedas. I am the subject of Veda.

How many life forms are there?

There are two types of beings known as Naswara and Anashwara. In the physical world every living being is perishable. In the spiritual world every being is nonperishable.

There is one superior to both known as Parameshwara who enters all three worlds since he is beyond Naswara and Anashwara. Since I am non-destructible (eternal) superior to Jeevaatma, I am known as Purushottama in all worlds and in the Vedas.

Arjuna! One who knows me as Purushottama without any doubt, one who meditates all the time as Parameshwara becomes a Jnani.

The Lord explained the Materialistic world comparing it with inverted Tree, an image of real tree at the bank of the water reservoir. The image is unreal. Does not last long gets disturbed with waves. When water evaporated the image disappeared. The roots of inverted trees are spreading towards sky, beyond which the origin lies for the tree. Real trees are spiritual.

Chapter 16

Daivaasura Sampad Vibhaga Yoga

Arjuna! Greed, anger, pride and ignorance are the attributes of demons.

Divine attributes lead to liberation, while demon attributes lead to bonding.

Arjuna! You are born with divine attributes so you will reach salvation.

Humans are of two types: one with divine attributes, and the other with demonic attributes

Divine Attributes:

1. Fearless
2. Purified soul
3. Spiritually knowledgeable
4. Control of the senses

5. Performing yagna
6. Possess Vedic knowledge
7. Practices penance
8. Practices simple living
9. Does not inflict pain on others
10. True to oneself.
11. Equanimous
12. Sacrifices for the greater good
13. Spreads harmony
14. Accepting of everyone
15. Kind
16. Courageous
17. Detachment to material possessions.

Demonic Attributes:

1. Not understanding their purpose.
2. Cannot differentiate right from wrong.
3. No faith in higher power.
4. Believing the only reason for their existence is to procreate.

5. Actions are malevolent in nature and promote harm to others.
6. Using the strength for the destruction of humanity.
7. Commit heinous activities.

Leading a life with demonic attributes is to lead a life without a moral direction.

Believing in supreme power gives the direction to lead a righteous life.

Doors to hell:

Desires, Anger, Greed are three attributes known as doors to hell. They cause destruction to Atman. One must work towards the renunciation of these three attributes.

Scriptures and Vedas are the standards that define our life's path. They are the compass that show us the right direction.

Chapter 17

Shraddha Traya Vibhaga Yoga

Arjuna asked Krishna, My lord! There are people who perform yajna, prayers with all devotion and as per scriptures. Is their faith Satvik?"

People are divided in three categories: Satvik, Rajas and Tamas. The lifestyle of a person depends on his internalization (Antah Karana).

Those with Satvik characteristics revere the devatas, those with Rajas idolize demons and those with Tamas worship ghosts.

The food ingested by Satvik promotes longevity, intelligence, health, strength, and happiness. Such foods include fruits, vegetables, dairy, grains, and lentils.

The foods that are bitter, sour, salty, and spicy are consumed by Rajasic people.

The food that is stale and not cooked properly are consumed by people with the Tamasic people.

Yajnas:

The yajna that is performed dutifully, solely to fulfil the practice as laid out in the scriptures and with a sense of purpose is known as Satvik Yajna.

The yajna performed for glory with a desire to be rewarded is known as Rajasic Yajna.

The Yajna that is performed with an uncaring attitude with no regard to the practice laid out in the scriptures is known as Tamasic Yajna.

Penance: Penance is of six types.

1. Serving the Gods, Brahmins, Teachers and Jnanis.

2. The speech that is used only for prayers, chanting mantras, and Vedas.

3. Practicing to attain equanimity, silence, self-control, and internalisation.

4. Performing all the above with dedication and without expecting any reward is called Satvik Penance.

5. Penance to attain glory and recognition is known as Rajasic Penance.

6. Penance that causes harm to others is called Tamasic Penance.

OM TAT SAT:

These words represent Parabrahma, from whom in the beginning of creation Vedas, Brahmanas, and Yajnas were developed. Hence, those who chant Veda mantras or perform yajnas, charity, penance in an orderly way, use this word of "OM" as a precedent.

Those who desire liberation, perform all these by reciting the word "TAT".

Those who have a feeling of truthfulness, feeling of supreme and before performing noble actions they recite "SAT".

When there is no intent or dedication, the actions are known as "ASAT".

Chapter: 18

Moksha Sannyasa Yoga

Arjuna: My Lord! I am eager to learn about renunciation and asceticism.

Lord replied, "Renouncing those actions which have desires is known as ascetism."

Disowning the benefits of actions is called renunciation. But all actions are to be sacrificed, as every action is done in self-interest.

Others say yajna, penance, and charity are the greatest forms of service to God.

<u>Reasons for performing actions:</u>

As per the Vedas, for the accomplishment of any action, there are five reasons:

1.Body 2. Subject 3. Practices (Instrument) 4. Effort 5. God

If a person does good or bad, the above five become the causes, but one who feels the soul as subject for all actions is innocent known as Ajnana. These people cannot recognise the truth.

It is impossible to accomplish detachment without eliminating the feeling of "I", "me" or "Mine "in every action.

Inspiration to action:

Janam — ability to apply wisdom.

Jnana — wisdom

Janata — scholar

These three attributes are needed to perform an action.

Jnani and Jnana:

The universe comprises millions of species. Those who recognise God dwell in the heart is known as Jnani. Such a Jnani would possess Satvik Jnana. He believes and trusts that he is merely an instrument for every action he performs with the influence of God. He practices the virtuous deeds as laid out in scriptures.

An egocentric person is in denial of God's dwelling in our hearts. Their knowledge is different from the Satvik Jnana and is called as Rajasic Jnana.

That knowledge which believes that the body is everything and all actions pertain to the body and not the mind and the soul is Tamasic Jnana.

Intellect:

As per scriptures, fulfilling the responsibilities using the intellect and implementing that intellect is known as Satvik.

The intellect that cannot differentiate between dharma and adharma, responsibility and irresponsibility is known as Rajasic Intellect.

The intellect that sees adharma as dharma, dharma as adharma is known as Tamasic Intellect.

Dhruti:

It is the determination and grit in a person that makes them strive continuously towards a goal. It is a quality of courage, patience, enthusiasm, and perseverance to face and overcome all odds and obstacles.

With dharana shakti (amazing abilities) and meditation which can control the mind, life force, senses, is known as Satvik Dhruti. He treats every action itself as GOD. He offers the fruit to the Lord.

The energy by which action is performed with Kama and attains moksha is known as Rajasic Dhruti. He performs all rituals with a desire.

The Dhruti by which one performs by yielding to the human emotion is called Tamasic Dhruti.

Happiness:

Satvik Happiness is the happiness derived from actions through self-realization, and it is everlasting.

Rajasic Happiness is the happiness derived through material means and is fleeting in its nature. This is temporary and harmful over an extended period.

Tamasic Happiness is the momentary happiness derived from instant gratification of worldly pleasures.

Humans cease to exist without these three attributes.

Social Division:

About three thousand years ago, the categorization of people based on socio-economic factors and their occupations led to the caste system. The product of that division created Brahmins, Kshatriyas, Vaishyas, and Shudras.

Superior intellect was attributed to this group of people called Brahmins.

The group was associated with leadership traits and valour and thus came the warriors from Kshatriyas.

Farming and trad ing came from this group called Vaishyas.

Wherever Krishna, the Yogeshwar, and the superior archer Arjuna both appears, there will be abundant wealth, victory, Unlimited energy and with no harm to morality.

This group did the manual labour called Shudras.

However, the Lord made it clear that you can be born into any caste. What determines your case is the attributes you possess. Thus, a person born as a Vaishya can be a Kshatriya if he/she exudes and practices the Kshatriya way of life.

How to accomplish divine state through self-realisation?

The basic reason for the existence of all life forms is the lord who is omnipresent.

Swadharma / Para Dharma

Swadharma is one's duty as an individual according to the Vedas. Swadharma is unique to every person as each of us have different capabilities. Executing the duties based on those capabilities is following their own dharmas. Arjuna is a warrior, and it is his duty to fight for justice and this is Swa-dharma.

Para-Dharma is the principle of following or executing someone else's duties. It is ideal to follow your own duties based on your calibre and not to fulfil others' actions no matter how simple or complex those tasks are.

One who has no interest in world affairs and by winning the self-consciousness with the nature of renunciation will attain success with no aim on the result of action.

How do you attain success through Jnana yoga?

The intellect becomes holy when it is pure. The self-realisation happens when one practices meditation, eats Satvik food, and gives up material desires and possessions. One can become a karma yogi.

How does one attain happiness and peace?

Offer all your actions to me wholeheartedly. Execute the action and make me your destination. You can overcome all your hurdles.

Arjuna!

Your nature is inspiring you to fight but your attachment is pulling you away from your Dharma. You are bound by your nature to perform the action for which you are employed. Lord remains with everyone in his heart as "Antaryaami" (who dwells in heart) and he alone can decide the movements of every being.

So, one who surrenders to the Lord, will attain peace and happiness. Thus, I am providing you with the most secretive Jnana. Internalize this and decide. Of all the wisdoms, listen to these divine sermons. You are my dear friend and hence I delivered the divine message. Keep your mind on me, be my devotee and offer your prayers to me.

You will attain me.

Leave all other Dharmas and surrender to me. I will liberate you from all sins.

What are the benefits of reading and listening to Gita?

Gita should not be taught to those who have no devotion, who do not practice penance or who do not have faith in the Lord. Whoever develops devotion to me, one who holds the secret to Gita in his heart will reach me. No one is greater than my devotee. No one is dearer to me than my devotee.

Anyone who has heard the sacred conversation between us (Lord & Arjuna) is equal to the one who performs Jnana Yajna and meditates by keeping their focus on me, said Lord Krishna.

Gita is the gateway to liberation. One becomes free from all sins and reaches divine worlds.

Partha! Have you listened to this science of Gita with a focused mind? Have you become free from ignorance and passion?

Arjuna replied: Krishna! With your blessings, I feel enlightened and can come out of the disillusion. I can perceive the world through different lenses, and I am ready to fulfil my tasks. I bow to you and will follow your orders.

Why is Sanjay Happy?

Sanjay witnessed the wonderful divine form of Krishna. He heard the conversation between Krishna and Arjuna, which is the most sacred of all. He was in awe of what he witnessed and what he heard, and he felt blessed.

Wherever Krishna is a charioteer, and Arjuna holds the bow called Gandiva, on a chariot, they will be blessed with victory. This is my opinion, said Lord Krishna.

Thus, Upanishad, Brahma Vidya, Yoga Shastra and the Bhagavad Gita, the conversation of Krishna and Arjuna, seeking Moksha Sannyasa Yoga with eighteen chapters are completed.

Think of me always and meditate on me, be my devotee, perform pooja t me. Bow to me. You are sure to get me as you become my affectionate friend, this is my promise.

OM TAT SAT – Gist of Gita

The Lord dwells in every being and in everything. He is omnipresent, The Lord dwells in every being and in everything. He is omnipresent, omnipotent

He will always be there for those who believe in him. He surrenders to his devotees.

The force behind modern science, engineering, technology, innovation, and humanity is Krishna.

Gita bridges the gap between understanding all the above disciplines and shows the path to lead a righteous life. This is where science meets spirituality.

Jnani says that God resides in us as infinite consciousness and is the force behind any action that we perform.

The body functions only because of the soul.

Who is behind every action? Jnani recognises the soul.

If the soul leaves the body, the body ceases to exist. The body is destructible while the soul is eternal.

Based on the actions (virtuous, sinful) performed, the subsequent birth is decided by the soul. This is the extract of Gita.

The actions of this life decide the birth or rebirth in our next life.

The absence of the very feeling of "I" in the execution of action with no expectation on the result but with the responsibility for accomplishment is the only way preached by Gita.

Meditation is the path prescribed which allows the practitioner to find the path of self-realization and realisation of the lord.

Cream of Geeta is explained in three slokas called as Samkshipta (Condensed) Geeta in 18th Chapter slokas 51-53.

Attaining the Lord requires us to have faith in the Lord, control over the senses, understand the Gita and relinquish the material possessions.

www.ingramcontent.com/pod-product-compliance
Lightning Source LLC
LaVergne TN
LVHW061617070526
838199LV00078B/7320